MW01716887

Now Is the Thing to Praise

Also by this author:

Through the Ceiling

Now Is the Thing to Praise

Poems

by

Dolores Kendrick

Detroit
LOTUS PRESS
1984

International Standard Book Number: 0-916418-54-5
Library of Congress Catalog Number: 83-82774

First Edition

Second Printing, March 1986

Grateful acknowledgment is made to *The Beloit Poetry Journal, Dasein, Freeing the Spirit, Nethula Journal, Open Places,* and *The Washington Review,* where some of these poems originally appeared.

Lotus Press, Inc.
Post Office Box 21607
Detroit, Michigan 48221
(313) 861-1280

In celebration of the God of Gifts . . . . .

. . . . and for my brother,
Bob, and for Paul Breman,
and for Robert Hayden, who
showed me where to find
the star when it closed.

Contents

So if your life trades its seventy years for
seventy hours I have that value now and am
lucky enough to know it. . . . . now is the
thing to praise and I am very happy with it.
Now, it has a funny sound to be the whole world
and your life. . . .

Ernest Hemingway
For Whom the Bell Tolls

I.

From Barcelona

Scattering
(for Lois Vrooman)

It was first the furniture:
removing it away from
the center of things,
farming it out,
wherever it could settle,
whomever it could serve.

Not important, not really
a matter of argument;
I must go: to another place,
another country, the language
of leaving familiar, needing
no translation outside
my eyes, my plans:

a surprise, this country.
Later the little boxes,
books, a collection of shells,
a fat rock my mother had
picked from the Colosseum
and labled "Rome" a year
before her death,

photographs, dishes, small
bells, paintings, sculptures,
finally, her piano, the only
thing she ever owned. It was
a diversement, a matter of duty,
a cleansing, a confession.
In scattering these matters

among my friends, what I had
sensed as a jarring, a fragmentation
of my smallest possible dreams,
an unrooting of noticeable
journeys moving in wood and cloth,
paint, stone, porcelain, and
textures took form away from me

in borrowed rooms, last annunciations,
adoptions. In the end, I could not
tell the difference.

Meetings

We Blacks
who live
in Barcelona

like to give
away our fears
to crowded streets

so peers
of another race
might give temporary

homage to our
kind. We face
that with a smile,

see each other
in slight passing
knowing all the while

our little hungers,
greet each other thinly
with our backs.

Shipping Curry

Distances deceive.
If the familiar is
left behind, it steals

and escapes like a thief.
The smell of curry hides
in my kitchen back home

and keeps me warm here
in my small apartment
on the Mediterranean,

in Barcelona, where
flowers drip over the
sides of balconies like

honey. It is all too
strange to fill me up.
There is a monster

somewhere in my Spanish
kitchen who likes to
break glasses and run

like hell. I want to find
her, sweep her up with my
broom, give her garlic for

answers. I need the familiar,
the Black child holy at the
gate, the smell of hot oils

dressing the chicken, the babel
of lazy friendships. Oh,
Barcelona is best at afternoon

when the sky is sticky
and the streets water
in the sun! But my

monster is close by,
in the narrow kitchen,
and my personal effects

have arrived at last
with the curry in a tin
strong and stubborn.

Un Peu de Noir

(for Cathy, Hans, and Rose)

My friend, who is waiting,
stands by the railway gate
in Geneva, waves Goodbye.

We are two women *de noir*
leaning in the brash light
small in our holdings

that attract the compulsive
and curious in a strange
and wintery land. People stare.

I leave her large welcome.
I have a little something
to say: I don't want to go,

I don't keep separations well.
Barcelona is two generations
up the road, and I am stranded,

growing older, vulnerable,
too alive. The eyes wet quickly,
the heart moves downhill like

a racer, the wrung indifference
is no longer kept. There is no
salon de espera in the dark,

no way station, just a deserted
corner made to be generous.
(For one must be generous

when in pain.) I am glad now;
I smile. I will miss the family,
the house, the familiar talk,

the small walks with young
Stephannie in the mountains;
such visits predict narrow

risks (no battles) and I let
go, or rather watch my friend,
who stands behind the iron gate

like a prisoner handling
leftover affections in the
seams of smiles and gestures.

She catches *un peu de noir*
in her outstretched hand,
holds it away from the light

so that I can bear the distance,
hear it hum and dance. It is
then that I know that nothing

is familiar, that everything
comes full circle in deep
and possible rings, that goodbyes

do not exist. *Le restaurant,
Madame? Vous voudriez manger?*
A waiter leans over my shoulder

as the train groans toward
Barcelona. No, Madame does
not wish to eat, the time

is ripe and fallen. The fruit
is sweet and good; lame meteors
have memories. Madame is not hungry.

Me Allegro

The lights are down,
there is music drifting
from the bedroom,

Ella, I think,
sweetening the burned
Spanish air that already

tastes of garlic,
gasoline, stale
cigarettes, the fresh

sea biting at the bottom
of the hill, the sun
in its throat. Somehow

the air manages to limp
through the open
bedroom window, fugitive

from the noisy streets.
Opposite my *piso*
an old lady, in a blue

bathrobe, looks down
over her balcony, checks
things out, as mellow

Ella sings over
Radio Dos and a caged
bird through something

holy swallows her song
and opens his.

Two

The Alhambra

Mohammed V:

The Emir builds
his rooms to start
the day with stars,
end it with the sun.

His Black imagination
sprouts stalactites
of gems from ceilings,
sews minerals of earth

from tops of rooms
calculated to delight,
the delicate and intricate
carvings of his language,
the blues and reds and golds
that will not sink away
in centuries of blood
and the ruins of history.

His Black footstep
does not vanish
in the sultry Mediterranean
but makes a bed beside it;
his first rich breath
warms Granada like the sun
while in his courtyard
of the lions, he prowls
the ages in singular
passion that endures
in stone and arch,
soft pool, pillar
and garden:

oleander, cypress, eucalyptus, myrtle.

For in these fragile rooms,
these sensuous spaces,
these reflections of his beauty,
are the measures of his dream,
his stout accomplishment,
his poem to God.

Now the keepers working
in his house, bathe his
smooth, rich skin,
keep his dream awake.

Now the tourist dares:

offers alms to Allah
because the Lion is asleep
and cannot be disturbed,
cannot sift the decomposing decade
from the dirt.

The Sagrada Familia

Antonio Gaudi:

He must have seen
him many times
as he held
the floating vision
in his eye.

Yes, the Emir
was his friend
his first agitation
and his final agony
that danced upon
his dream.

He wanted all.
Everything.
No giving of
a sacrifice
but something
stronger, strange,

unwoven in his past,
in his first and final
destiny.

Only the Arab would do:

only the blood
of the Black man
whose veins
he carried,
whose heart
was his, and tongue.

He found the stalactite
melting from the Arab's sky,
falling in air,
whispering,

this Spaniard who was yet
to mark his time
reached up and found
the Moor dancing, Black
and ripe, in bloom,
full in his juices.

He called
and found his echo
bearing him upward,
whole, without bone
for a balance,
without death.

So he became the Moor's heir,

his only blood
without a conquered
race. He reached up
again, saw the sky
hung in steeples,

poured Hosannas
into doorways
that opened to clouds.

Before the last
melting Sanctus
struck the sky,
he would go
to meet his Arab
brother, lie
beside him
in the moonlight,
talk of stars
and God.

Paco de Lucia at the Palau de Musica

He didn't bring
the music
to the guitar,

he put the song
the irreverent note
the wail, the siren

the magnificent thrust
of anguish into it.
His was the body

the guitar sang through
and you could see it,
as he writhed and jumped

closed his eyes
held the instrument
to his chest, as though

when the beat ended
his heart would burst.
Maybe it did, or tried,

as he rumbled the last
Flamenco note to
a high ecstasy

that had no way
to come down,
so he hung it there

dangling in the air
with no place to drop.

And he left it levitated,
weightless, for the audience
to climb into.

And when his entire ensemble
came onstage, three other
guitarists (one sang Flamenco)

a flutist and a drummer, why

that last man was Black

and when he pushed
those bongoes into
the Spanish Blues

the music rose,
found debris on the moon,
cleaned it up, tossed it

into the fire of the night
and made stars of the ashes.
This Black man, sitting on

his wooden drum, white heat
in his fingers, a memory
for collusions, for the secret

heritage

keeping the faith
as only he could:

walking into sound:
coming out burning.

The Bar at Muntaner

The shudder of coffee
greets me as I enter.
Hola! Buenos días!

The woman behind the bar
opens my day, though
the day has been tight

and narrow, though
the day has grown
wrinkles and looks

like an old woman
deaf, with too many
silences struggling

in her brain, but the
woman behind the bar
opens my day with her

magic key all the same.
I order a hot tea,
with lemon, and while

I sit on my low stool
under the window, the bar
awning outside lingers

in the sun, something
flesh about it, something
soft when exposed, the sun

a customer arriving at three
with me, with my hands
stretched for the cup,

with the hot tea warming
my tongue, my mouth
and the lemon sun, thick

and large. I glance at
the *postres* and look
away to rows of glasses

and wines. Can't afford
the sweets. None today.
None tomorrow. None

yesterday. Only the
sounds of voices from
the other room, sweetening

the rich expresso air.
These bars are ancestors,
blood-lines. It takes

at least a century
for the ceilings to dim
and the light to quicken

for the woman making
the sandwiches and coffees
and teas and drinks

to run upon her bed
without her lover
in the shoals of her

breasts, without her cleft
smile warming her rooms
and feasts, for the customers

to drain their cups,
the rooms to melt,
the songs to finish,

the sun to vanish
and leave its ghost
for a small winter tip.

II.

Now Is the Thing to Praise

Now is the Thing to Praise

And Paris: The Albino with his hair dyed black walking across
the Boulevard Voltaire, and Black the grey-haired woman, slow
and definite, her step to the curb as sure as the arch of her small
back, the gift of her smile, her legs yawning through traffic.
And Nicola, Collete, Raphael whispering in French in the evening
corners of their rooms, the quiet gentility of their smiles warming
the air, the cold, rainy night flickering beyond the windows, the
African spontaneity of welcome greeting whatever is with a kind of
laughter that breaks and eases and slips into light hours we call
time, strong loving we call ritual, bodies lithe and comely,
bone born in the first thoughts of civilization. Colors obey them.
They are Masters, Lords, Ladies, Royalty around a great table
that wears an orange cloth, some bread and salad, potatoes, baked
sheepshead, oranges. Where the blood roots from African sun, their
kingdoms stride little edicts of welcome to the stranger, and the
souring lonely land that is just now beginning to rot on the bush.

The patisserie with brass-ringed tables, sweet brioches with raisins, hot
tea with lemon; the crowd stuffed into the Café de la Paix, the shallow
tables and groaning floors listening to feathery conversations carelessly
dropping in the air, little glasses of brandy (always with a cube
of sugar) that sit like tiny computers on small round pedestals,
storing the liquid erosion of milky faces, swaying smiles, a curve
to the laughter, a pull to the appetite. Faces line up like birds
on a high wire. Will it come? The first shock that means a hot-like
death that freezes? Never to pull oneself out of an awkward position,
a fantasy, never to know what the next move might be, what the next
sound could tell? But the heavy cigarette smoke makes them invisible.
Only now and then an etching of an eye in the corner, or a mouth
poised to speak . . . And the waiters walking tightropes, watching the
charades and annoyances, taking tips half-consciously (it is a game)
knowing that the greying fat man with the lovely young girl by
his side will get up soon, somewhat abruptly, and push ten francs
into one of their hands for the same table in the corner next time.

The ballet has begun. An Arabesque by the table of the old woman dressed in black, an amethyst at her throat. Places, places everyone, please! Three claps of the hands. A Chopin prelude will do. Three young men dance by and disappear down the Rue de la Paix, and a tall skinny fellow, camera over his shoulders peers over the lip of the café, watches for an unsure face, in his head, counts the money and the change. Pas de deux!

Oh, days of lingerings and strange self-warnings throbbing in the images of salient streets! Oh, streets of sweet mornings that start before they begin! Oh, little beginnings of pretty things laughing at friendships and lovers and careful paradises found! Oh, sirens found of last night's whisperings carrying the dead to their last tables! Oh, tables of feasts and visions of hot distances yet to be touched, yet to be moved, always to be held soft in sunlight, in the past midnight of the last moon, in the milk of stars and manageable dreams!

She, great in the bones, large and homely threatened by the Black woman moving about the edges, the latitudes and longitudes, the jet-streams and high pressure systems. Storms. He, little French man, liberal by liberties, winds and gales, changes in weather, low pressures, rain and sun in the same moment, long, long sweet silences over the years, downed to twenty, too long for friendships, too short for whatever matters, nothing in between, only letters and visits and notes and telephone numbers and aspirin and empty wine glasses and the last string of well-wishing words, though his lover-woman while in their intellectual bed found Black too much her shame because the contrast exposed too cruelly the limp in her smile. Clear day! Have a good one!

James Baldwin chatting over a brandy on the Champs Élysées, a rainy day, the cold scratching like pins, the dark grey avenue awash with cars, the quiet genius of his meandering thoughts, his deep strong eyes and rich smile that has the courage to enter upon dark rooms and mouldy afternoons. Two Black men strolling by, recognizing, entering, honoring, a few words, a few gestures, a few handshakes, one wearing a blue face, too black to be black, only the strength of unmixed blue can hold it; the other, cape thrown about his shoulders cavalier style, kissing hands as he moves toward the door, outside around the corner, glancing through glass, bowing his way into the rain and the cold hours that found him somewhere in the dying streams. And Baldwin, hoping for a taxi in the crowds: "We'll be late," he says of his reception waiting on the Right Bank. "But," and he looks at the surly clouds and sour weather, "everybody's late today."

The young boy singing lullabies wildly to subway walls at Montreuil, a wilder bag lady answering in threadbare notes and ragged tones. And Angers: Jean Lucrat, the awesome *le chant du monde*, a song of tapestry pouring from Gothic walls; the vision: *do not be surprised to find gall and honey . . . . l'homme en gloire dans la paix, l'eau et le feu, champagne la poésie,* rhythms, counter-rhythms, dissonances, études, tone-poems, concertos, blues, ballads, jazz, twelve-tone scales, operas, ballets, under it all a chant of creation ringing around a brilliant chant of color moving into lush indulgences, deep sunsets, while the light is sweet and passing, so dying, so red in its inhabitance, so blood-pounding, so deep in flesh and sweat, so strangely sinking, so matter-of-fact in the dark, so pausing and quick, so gone, so strong before the final contradiction.

Oh, trees that find no weather for a root! Oh, root that grows out of the moon! Oh, moon that leaks before it rises! Oh, risen things now pouring in the dark!

It is Lucrat's darkness that is benevolent; it is his universe that brings a celebration from tender, stricken, unfamiliar things. It is his beauty that overcomes the night!

And Barcelona: Flamenco and the Blues, Billy Holiday howling
through electronic skin, notes edging like escalators downward, steps
into pain catching the bizarre in a syllable, rounding afterwards
in circles of twisting floating wounds, she squeezing the pus from
the poison, only the healing to be done, to be finished, to be let go
in one, sweet, shivering sound that can't even make a word . . . Newborn
leaves from the wombs of young trees, birth-songs tender in the new light.
The Mediterranean, the smell of scallops along its ribs, the figure
in a small boat, far out into the water, smoothly rowing from space
to space. And night. The beach asking ablutions.

The gypsy walking across the square at the Paseo de la Gracia,
his back harnessed with all he owns, a fat brown puppy in his
rough arms, sherry in Señora Vilalta's apartment, the bold crystal
bottle on a table distorted by the path of a civil war bullet,
something remembered, graced, something in the flute-player
at the subway entrance of Plaza Catalunya, something of enigma
in Monserrat, a rock of cloud hiding in a rainy fog, something
in a mountain supper in cold white air and vineyards
at the feet of *el palacio de los ventos*, the palace of the
winds, testing the rich blue sky, supper at the long table,
salad, olives, fish, sausages, Spanish tortillas, wine, bread,
flan, something in the high stretch of valley as it rises
in rich mountains of white grapes, something in the
laughter of the winds as it pauses, takes notice of an afternoon
melting into its fruit.

Something in the Now.

*Oh, last coming leaning on stars! Oh, first coming eating
into sun! Oh, little dreams crawling in the grass! Oh, journey
into Now! Oh, fever of distances! Oh, listenings! Oh, mystery!
Oh, syllables of light!*

And coming home: the parish church where once we were kept
to the back pews, the silence of shadows, the spiritual witness,
now, the new church with a new skin (a Black Christ) a restora-
tion of an old ethic through a new pastoral voice, a new
solemnity, an old forgiveness raging on its brow, a lonely
song yet to be sung, but someone to sing it in a gentle
woman whose "sound" gives the church's emancipation a sweetness,
whose great, striding voice teases, exalt, lullabies the old,
tired history, eases Jesus into the back pews like He was
just coming from Golgotha.

And I: the choirloft holding me too suddenly, opening tired
wounds because I remembered my childhood in that loft and
those pews from which we made our prayers in a trust stronger
than the damaged litanies of our white brothers. And I:
holding an awful time in my eye for a quick moment as
I moved across the loft to share a celebration of a woman's
great voice. And I: in mid-air, stunned, wanting to cry,
wanting to lift myself away from all that pain and all that
Past. And I: finding their ghosts stilled in the pausing
pews, knowing they were surely the true élite, smiling,
gracious, leaning upon their fine endurances, the wealth
of their witness, their celebrations of longer matters.
And I: remembering, feeling the tether of a shrine no one
had built, but there, in the slow church hum. And I:
dazed, restored, brought to my beginnings, in joy.

Oh, syllables of light!

III.

The Women of Plums

All on a Note

(for Sarah Vaughn)

The bass
bothers
throws in
a word
but she
recovers,
takes the downbeat
into her
chest,
heaves
it like
soft storms
into high
altos
of air;
sounds
through pain
and prayer
command:
send in
the clowns . . .

Canticle of a Black Lady

dying asks a question: she gives an answer

Done. Every ounce of it. Fly winds to sea-rocks and break
a round of prayer upon their backs.

Turtles, take notice! You may walk with your eyes upright.
Beasts in the forest, part the noon with your cries.
Stretch your bones into the sun, embrace Amen as you eat the air.

It is done! Said. Pronounced. Motioned. Spoken. Astonished.
The men of oranges have shed their skins and their flesh is puffed
upon weeds. The women of plums are sweet and black. Their flesh
is moist with tears of joy! Their dreams are skins the color of dusk.
Their ripe dreams bitten into leave a sour sweetness in the membranes
of the mouth.

The children of quince quiver in the womb; their eyes are dowries,
their tongues, soft songs.

And the Bride comes forth carrying peacocks upon her fingers, bearing
roses in her hair. She comes forth beyond the wedding-day and speaks
I will and *Amen.*

Two Poems: for Diana Lodge

I.

The lone wolf also shall dwell with the lamb

1. Whatever the world
propels in us
or demands or forsakes

makes little sense
unless we come forth whole;

bye and bye
the first summer
stings our wantonness

in the hollows
of our rootless smiles;

and the leopard shall lie down with the kid

we need only
to lie down a little
our backs of prayers
bruising our lips.

Once a Woman
put her song to fire
and blew out the rage
of centuries with
one single breath:

so must all women in the end;

all mothers, wives,
sisters and daughters

and the calf and the young lion and the fatling together

flesh into flesh
bone from narrow bone
in the hill
in the shadow.

2. There are Black Virgins
all over Europe
crowned and stunning

smiling from the great
cathedrals growing out of
the backs of their souls,

and in Black Africa
they sit upon
the Apocalypse

cooking sheepshead for dinner
while the wolf is lonely
and the leopard follows the calf,

and a little child shall lead them.

II.

I have seen
monasteries
in Spain

in Mexico
and Greece
in the quiet

fields of America
listening to tender
chants in the sun,

but your soft cottage
in the Slad, under the
English hills

in the choirs
of the quince trees
and the lilac

and the magpie
and the lamb
and the cloister

of young grass
that waves in the wind
like the sea,

striking shoreward
as once these Cotswolds
knew, as once their

drowning came to light,
surfaced again,
remembered, stayed,

as once the ghost sea
visits through the land,
as these winds, as this grass

gives death to nothing,
drinks, but ceases
to drain: yes, I have seen

monasteries in all this,

the kind you go to
in the next village,
the kind that make

prayer out of water.
And I have seen
them climbing

eighty years of your bone,
like chapels, like rituals,
like the limestone you live in.

Solo: the good blues

(for Alberta Hunter)

long way from the whorehouse
to the White House
long song long gone
gone when I was twelve
stretching to thirteen
stretching to thirty,
fifty, long eighty

aint no whorehouse
can hold a holy girl
aint no whorehouse
can hold a holy girl
it's the song that matters
nothing else in this world

get me to Paris
get me a name
get me (if you can)
in the long note game!

tell me your trouble
tell me your sin
just call me Woman
I'm your next-of-kin:

write off the lonely
write off the sad
my dream's a hurtin'
my sorrow's had!

ain't no whorehouse
can hold a holy girl
ain't no whorehouse
can hold a holy girl
it's the song that matters
nothing else in this world

wide way from the whorehouse
to the White House
wide from girl to Woman
deep and wide from little
Black girls who had a song
but nowhere to sing it
except whorehouses
long and deep and wide

thank you, mr. president,
my, this house is big,
it almost fills my throat!

my God! What a morning!

my long Black God!
we made it! and I'm
the living proof!

hold the holy, hold the holy girl
hold the holy, hold the holy girl
take her in an octave
and give her to the world.

Sister Jessie

(for Juanita)

Jessie came swaying down the aisle,
her fat body was her sanctuary
and she was proud to show it.

I wanna be happy
I wanna be happy
I wanna be happy
Walkin' Jerusalem
Jes lak John!

Her hips swung, her heavy legs
sank into shoes that were
flat enough to give her support.

I wanna be happy
I wanna be happy
I wanna be happy
Walkin' Jerusalem
Jes lak John!

Down the aisle she danced,
the other choir members swishing
to her beat, catching Jessie's
high notes in their throats,
giving them away like water.
Her voice was high bright Black

with a dimple in the side of one
note. Her hair was white grey,
as if to give the shine of smooth skin

tasting her face a decent Hallelujah.
Lord! Lord! Jessie cried as she
began to clap her hands, as the whole

congregation rose and clapped their
hands, too, making sure they didn't
miss Jessie's rhythms by an upbeat

or a down. "Come singing, Sister
Jessie!" someone shouted from the
fifth row front, and Jessie kept

coming until the aisle was finished
and she looked neither sideways
nor backward, just shut her eyes

and kept clapping and coming until
the aisle was finished. When she
got to her seat in the front row

of the choir, the others followed
as she clapped and sang them
straight in. Together all those

women were a joyous bunch!
When the communion came,
she wept; her face lost

the smoothness and her eyes
got too soft for the air,
so she squeezed them

and rocked herself to Jesus,
who everybody knew looked up
from Jessie's lap.

. . . . wanna be . . . !

Three Poems for Gwendolyn Brooks

1. Sketch

Is the moment conscious that (with public prescription)

Black Runnymedes
and murdered hope
stretched to the root of my thumbs

tranquilized strokes any sleep

with holy pits of memory
like yesterday's dying. . . .
Shoveled into my loin

like lions, crust with Black men's grief,

this grief: the howl from mocking rain and gritty sun
and runny haze like pus; my crisp and sudden summer
blooms in syllables of blood. . . .

and lies humped in my house with a grunt of history

2. The Agony and the Bone

Chicago shanks . . . . .
hung along the lake
like churches; the rib awake

the groin of fasted days
for Lazaruses raised
from shanty towns, a phrase

of her like stitching wounds can make;

raw, the freshly killed alone
the young obscenity of home

weaning in the streets
the sacrificial bleats
of slaughters, meats

for mayors. She like love: the agony and the bone

3. **Interview in Color**

Did poetry
choose you
or was it
the other way
through?
And if so
where did
the two
of you
meet –
on a
vermilion street
near the
South Side El
or taupe
in pain
where *Endymion*
fell?

Black Women at the Basin

(for Ogretta and Kingsley)

Never were they abandoned.
They stood at the Basin
with wings in their throats

and brought their children
absolutions (though they knew
how to fly). And while

their men screamed in their
dreams, these women, stung
with imagination and ripe

belonging, opened their wombs
and brought forth fire, water,
earth, sea and air, took

the hurricane to their breasts
and singing ate the afterbirth
in order to keep the house whole,

unmolested, pure, without
violation or shame. They
were neither saints nor sinners

(never were they abandoned)
and they managed their horrors
in orderly conditions, with

a little grace, a bit of wisdom
struggling in their faces
and their smiles, as they asked,

And how are you today?
and *where do you come from?*
and *will the rain come or*

will it just be falling weather?
and *have you had your supper?*
The Basin lies clean now, pure,

because they are gone and no one
wants to put her dirt into
a holding-place, a ciborium

of sacred things, a container
that, in the end, only manages
to cast a reflection.

For Madelyn

In the kitchen
by the hanging fern,
the Swedish ivy
and African violets

she moves about
by the great windows
curved to the bright
room, serving, through
their partly open mouths

a cream of afternoon
sun. The pot is
yet to be stirred,
the sauce for spaghetti
stews and waits.

Her eyes wipe the table
(five for dinner)
then search for something
forgotten: perhaps the pepper
or the butter, the salad oil,

or the new wine glasses,
best for a Saturday supper
with old friends.
The antipasto, complete
with mozarella, sausage,

sardines, onions, rich
green olives, smelling
of garlic (from Naples)
anchovies, opens the meal
and the promises

and the sifting comforts
and the creed of her belonging.

Then the soup,
the spaghetti,
sweets, coffee
(the special almond).

She takes little notice
of ravenous hungers.
To her they are natural,
to her the awesome
appetites that bite

into her day,
her small privacies
that she no longer
can afford, are her

bound realities
laid by, put in little
jars with labels on them,
while she roots the myrtle
tree in her young garden

and thinks of how
the bamboo spreads
without the need
of her energy.

Alone, she is the first woman
scratching at the tree

where Yes is seed.

Jesus, Looking for an Aspirin

(for Erma)

Teaching,
making waves,
seeing, touching
the eye of the
hurricane

being swallowed
in the retina

coming back
alive, body burning
in meteors, hands
deep in pillars
of salt.

Once a woman
came too near

wanted to touch
to know the purity
of the turbulence
of death, wanted
the fire inside

her house, her breasts,
her groin, wanted a

lean master growing
from her eyelids.
Don't touch me, Jesus
smiles, I haven't gone
home yet. It's there

that the fire is clean
and leaves no ashes.

Right now I've a moment
to revive from rising,
the coming forth, the
death, I want to see friends
(you're the first)

and I need an aspirin.

She did not touch him.
(It was an unnecessary
gesture.) She merely
kissed the ground
he walked on

became his courier
relieved the headache.

Heritage

Great Grandmother Merriweather
left outside in the cold
by her son's anger
no other home
except death;
she goes there
confidently

Young Grandmother Hattie
dancing onstage
lithe Black body
slipping through
saxophones
tender and sweet
next morning
a show in Chicago

Elegant Aunt Lula
working as a housekeeper
rings on her fingers
combs in her hair
dusting parlors
with her
New England eyes

Old Mrs. Marshall
surrogate grandmother
strong and eighty-two
standing by the stove
making vegetable soup
dumplings and tea
talking Republican

Grandmother Merriweather
reaching through iron gates
to steal her children,
wards of the state,
missing their grasp,
drugged by her piano,
disappearing

Four Poems in Celebration of My Mother

I.

Josephine in the Jeu de Paume

My mother sitting in a hard sill
of light unlocking the room

of soft treasures to her Sunday
eyes: the Cézanne vase still as

air, set beside its reproduction
oozing blue-white oils into the

nostrils of her mind; filling
the pit of her hand and the palm

of her black and curious eye.
She delights at the sight of what

was and Will Be and watches
motionlessly the art of motion

stilled by a metaphor. She cannot
speak. The ghost of herself is but

a gesture of quiet light that she
alone controls, she only can see.

Distantly, she smiles and rises.
Outside, old men in black berets

and dry skins walk humming
in deep-pebbled sun.

II.

Working for Chopin

Étude #3 in E Major

It was while the water
was boiling in the kitchen
and the Beef Wellington
stretched in the cave

of crust so carefully
the woman you worked for
failed to see your thumbprints
stuck at the sides of the loin:

your trademark,
(no pretenders, please)

that you knew it was all
finished, these meals made
for strangers, this giving
of your tender talent that

nowhere fit the little weekly
paycheck stuck into your purse
as something of a compensation
for services borrowed

(sometimes swindled: almost stolen).

It was all over: the rest was
just theatre, stage, murmurs:

Breakfast at eight,
Lunch at twelve-thirty,
Tea at four,
Dinner at seven:

Codes and quandries having
nothing to do with your own
celebration of the life you
carried so delicately

in the body of your orphaned music.
Your children were strong,
alive, not wanting, and at your
table were linen cloths and flowers,

your normal way of life. And you
had your Baby Grand, the only thing
you owned.

So one day while something
sat cold on that same kitchen
stove, you took your paycheck
to a record shop and bought
all the music Chopin ever wrote.

Étude #4 in C Sharp Minor

The hours were
six to ten
time off
on Thursdays.

Sometimes
twenty
for dinner.

Sometimes the smell
of raw onions
in the pantry:

the sound of dreams
in the throat.

Now the needle
moves across
the record

circle into
circle
lifting
a piano

into a melody
made way back
before the storms
of Africa,
Portugal
(some blood there)

or Poland
or Paris

before hours
were accents
to reckon with
to survive by:

and the melody jumps
makes its way
obediently

beside the mumbling stove

to commands,
strange orders

sharp in C
all the way
through

in her.

On the record jacket
she writes: Chopin/
property of
Josephine M. Kendrick,

Gaga.

III.

The Snow Bird

Dressing the tree at Christmas
was her way of saying
some things
don't matter: scary nights when
the next day's food
would be
in somebody else's stomach,
not hers or the children's
don't matter.
Little crumbs of dreams lying about
in dark beds and broken
eyes
don't matter. A husband gone,
a life, a little stretch
of sun
drained in spots of unloving
don't matter. What matters
are the lean
rituals of morning dreams when
they smoke in the pit
of her hand,
scatter to her tired arm, extend,
swivel back into
her throat
giving it dry song as she reaches
for the string of small
white lights.
If the bulb is gone, out,
she knows the whole
shimmer
of Christmas night to come,
like the snow bird,
will rise
into her lyric wing of moving
hope, balancing on
narrow
windowsills and white evenings.
When the tree is finished,
she takes
the ritual of her warm brown
body and dances on limbs
of hungry ice.

IV.

Catching Water

The woman in the park gave the child
an orange: *Take it, she said,*
and pull the skin before you eat,

but don't forget to save
the skin for Sundays:
it's the best day for eating skins.

When I was a child,
I went to bed with my mother
in my arms. Her dark skin

was like rich water breaking
through ice with sun
sealing in her smiles and

annoyances for me to touch
and wonder about. Catching her joy
in my arms (for she was always in

my arms) was like catching water
just before the skin breaks
and what is held within gives

and runs away. Her sculptured brown
voice was something I could handle
on the best of days and the worst

of nights, because it was clear
and stunning and plain as clay,
like skin, like water.

Take the juice first, the woman
said to the busy child,
then eat the flesh; but don't

be too surprised when
you eat the skin and
find it sobbing.

My mother died that orange day.
They buried her in rain she caught
rising in her rich and Sunday skin.

IV.

Other Matters

To My Soft Gone Friends

Nancy

In the wood
she sits and
swallows the stars.

Out of the climb
of the sun, she
stretches her eyes

knowing that,
if she dares,
a blindness

will embrace her
soon. The stars
are too rich

for her appetite,
but she knows how
to digest them.

Her husband waits
at the water's edge.
He watches the gulls

eat from the river.
There is no wind
today and the water

is soft and fragrant.
He wonders about
reflections and

the gull's wing
that barely
touches the water

as it rests upon
an image that
it shatters.

She has had enough.
She is full.
She knows the sun

will soon come
killed and in dying
turn the wood to bone,

hurry to the river,
sip it a little
to break the fever,

and bury itself
in its own ashes.
But she will be

blind by then
and her stars
will rattle

in her eyes.
She reaches
forward, finds

the river
suddenly swelled
ready for feasts

and rituals,
and her husband
waiting in the

dumb dark,
touching water,
drowning.

Virginia

When I see kitchens,
I think of Virginia,
her life in her hands
like warm bread
or the mushrooms
she scrubbed
with a special brush

so that their whiteness
would not sour in the
dark. Her cancer
(she owned it,
it did not own her:
she saw to that!)
had by then eaten
into her breasts
with more malice
than she had ever
known from anything
in the world she loved,

as though the disease
were jealous that she
could survive with such
grace while its foul breath
was upon her,

she, woman of kitchens and salt,

mother of a family of quail
that came to her garden
with quick accuracy of instinct
for daily meals; (we could
tell time by their arrivals).

In her suffering
she saw the world as
young, unspotted
as her unsoiled rooms
now standing alone
fetching shadows
instead of laughter
and peaceful conversation;

her kitchen of stews
and roasts, scallions,
tomatoes, plums,
watermelons, cakes,
puddings and cantaloupes
lingered in the house
like little ghosts
daring not to bite
or blow upon the season:

her meals were her ablutions.

We ate them hungrily
never knowing of the murder
moaning in her bosom
or the funeral pausing
in her eye.

That last summer
the mountains behind
her garden burned,

as if for her

as if to heal
her waiting.

Frank Pohlhaus

Steal away
Steal away
Steal away

1.

to Jesus

Steal away
Steal away home
I ain't got long

to stay here

Where did it all go?
The withering of the dream,
the wretched shadow
sitting cross-legged
on the court-room floor?

2.

The lawyer's lot
has its dimensions,
its dry finishings;
it isn't always
money.

Sometimes it is passion,
a little ugly egg
cracked on the table;
the children's whispers
in the raw rooms.

Where did it all go?

Whose rights are civil?
(Isn't that a bit redundant?)

I watched your drained
jaw when the last case
was down, when the land

fled into the law and found
it could not move because
3. its roots refused to rot:
a thing of energy, of seed,
a thing you knew.

You understood.

And when a white man
becomes Black because
that is the only way
to fight the good fight
and that is the only

4. way to be human
and that is the
only way to cry havoc
and feel the shingle
under the skin,
the stranger in the
flesh, to know
the pure taste

of the prophet's gall
and find the bitterness
in his next of kin,

then such a man
counts the catching
of his days (slipping
in the night); takes
his whiteness

from his dresser drawer
on the loneliest of occasions,
smiles when his Blackness
surfaces in white places

forcing him to a larger struggle

cleansing an ascent.

I celebrate you, Frank:
There was beauty in your gift,
which not even people
with the NAACP could know;
5. but it was quick,

quicker than the speed of sound.

By the time we heard it,
you were gone.

Delores

You had the voice
but not the ambition.
The church choir

was good enough. Within
the *Panis Angelicus* came
the lonely adagios

of fat childhood
that would someday
come to claim your

voice when you weren't
looking because
you died in the middle

of your song while
the note hung
warm and narrow

in mid-air. I believe
afterward you reached up
and brought it down

struggling as it came
so that those of us
who loved you

wouldn't be frightened.
I was in Paris,
bought you

from the Rue Rivoli
a scarf, something
silk and sweet

and soft to wear
next to the skin.
(Travelling gifts

are always the best.)
I thought remembering
you in Paris

would be good since
you remembered me
and mine there

and in Yugoslavia
where the air is warm
and Mexico

where gods sleep
in stone and Russia
where you found

palm trees and God knows
where else. What does
it matter?

All the quick while
you were dead.
Your songs sang

without you.
How did I know
that from Paris

I was bringing you
a shroud, sweet
next to the skin?

Marea

In that room you looked at me and said *When are you going to get married*
Around you was madness   nurses carrying lanterns to those who already saw
a special light   I lifted myself away   out of the energy of your past
into my own   the bright girlhood fastening itself to little days of
laughter where often there was none   the visit our families gave us to
Martha's Vineyard and how you saved me from a high sea one night after we
wandered too far over the beach's deep sandwall into the dark   Our Lents
Our Easters   Our young resurrections   Your own marriage   Children   The
last going of childhood that could no longer look forward to or remember
or care about the loneliness that was to come   The isolation   The fear
The one becoming Two and Three and Four   The stretching out of lives
from one who kept her dreams wrapped in linen   safe   and out of sight
so as not to disturb the sleep of strangers   *Soon*   I said   *but not now*

I must be ready   Marea   You're never ready   you said   *But remember   You mu*
wear my wedding gown   I've saved it for you   In your madness your little
space of light is pure   unviolated   Mine is murky and I have papers
of sanity   I can prove it   See   Marea   I show them to you now as I
sit beside you in this room that cannot contain either you or me   as I
dangle in darkness offering you kind words and well-balanced gestures when
I walk the tightrope between phrases of *get well* and *take care of yourself*
knowing that my balance is more precarious than yours   that you have familied
what I write poems about   But you're too thin and I've gained a little weight
The waste   Marea   you know   the waste within   Save the gown for me   friend
but don't smile   We need the right monsters to keep us sane

Rooms

I.

I don't know where it was. It was near,
where all the rooms were clothed in ice
and naked children walked beside me
and asked for candy.
That's not nourishment, I said.

II.

It was near. Their white bodies were
hot with fevers. I took their temperatures
and wondered if white flesh held heat
longer than Black. They wondered at my
curiosity.

III.

I walk into the classroom
with Baldwin, Brooks, Wright and Hayden,
their mastery of the universe,
the strut of their language
soft in my footprints.
I am filled.

IV.

And when I walk into the classroom,
I close the closet door at the end
of the room, look at the straight,
white teeth in the white mouths
of the white faces before me,
and pick up Shakespeare.

V.

Because I am different. I am
strangely-cultured. I know the land
that seeds the straight, white teeth,
where bloom the rooms of white mouths.
I discovered it long before Columbus;
I carried it in my loins while the
rivers of Africa swept through my blood.
I ate it when I was hungry, spat it out

when it sickened me; my children
sucked its swollen bosom. When the land
was dry, I caught its dust and made fragile
dreams when Shakespeare was but a thought.

I pick up Shakespeare. His body cracks.
The room grows larger.

VI.

So fine! This Black child standing
cold in the light of the old
schoolroom.
Public.

VII.

He is shivering. So am I.
One day I will leave him abruptly
(and I do not believe in violence)
while he screams quietly in
a corner, watching my blackboard
magic, noticing the dust on my heels.

VIII.

There's not enough room for us both.

We both have to grow.

We both need visions.

We both owe debts.

Yours a penny.

Mine a profession.

Pay up.

IX.

Those rooms were wild and funny:
but I left them because they starved me.
They were close and muggy and wet:
but I left them because they drained me.
They were narrow and dim and soft:
but I left them because they crushed me.
They were raw, infected, diseased:
but I left them because there was a stench
from the children's decaying spirits.

And in the doorway, blocking my
departure, stood three shapes with
white teeth, even and straight
(no braces) whispering to me:
Shakespeare! Shakespeare!

X.

Well, I have arrived.

XI.

English class. Nine AM. Private.
The sun is clear, the grass glistens.
In the quad the sky bothers to cloud
making quick shadows for the willow,
the birch and the elm. The skin
of the bright room itches: it always
seems to need lotions, creams, salves,
balms. It is very delicate. I wonder
if power is delicate, ever, if those
who live in fragile rooms become
the bones of such rooms; if all
the broken limbs that hobble through
the marble halls are diplomas of
unpitiable pride. (The stench again.)

XII.

I, too, have a power struck from
the lineage of my visions that crowd
upon me more demandingly than the dead
who walk me now. Their ghosts are
in their children, the white mouths,
the little questions. But these faces
are icons. They are gilden. They are
sweet and bloom in special rooms
in the right temperature and light,
while my visions knock at the door.

XIII.

Exeunt Ghost.
Shakespeare should know better.

Nevada: Going Through the Center

(to Frank D., III)

There are flatlands here
and sweet mountain clover.

We go through the circle
of mountains that are as

stunning as stillness
when they hold the ring

of land so clearly that
their flesh is soft enough

to kiss. Here the sky
is richly cerulean, fresh,

alive. Here it surrounds
and opens and grows wider

whenever there is another
house built or another car

driven. Our car is heavy
and glides along the road

as if it were a hand slicing
through water. But it's only

a car trying to be noiseless
in the middle of something that

gathers, empties, embraces,
breaks the horizon with a motion

that no ordinary machine
could ever recognize.

We travel like this for hours.
We are in the center of things

that hold, tighten, as a magnet
of open valley pulls us into

the honeyed air. Now, the car
is motionless, the motor

collapses softly and is drawn
by strange forces that know

the order of big and little
machines with borrowed power.

The secret is to surrender.
Beside the road are three llamas,

standing like storks, watching
strangers, little songs in their

eyes. We pass by. The green
is in the air, and the mauve

and the yellow that leaks in
the sun. Going through is easy.

We don't look back because
circles are like salt.

The Loss of Little Things

(in memory of my mother
and the Heathmans
and all their kind)

In those days the Island was as strange as widows' walks,
the sea like lions swallowed up the sand
shrinking beaches to cliffs and mounds
leaving just enough ground to walk or lie upon.
People came from eastern places, wrung their cars
like clamdiggers into the sandy roads, and sat upon the sea,
or knelt into it or struck within it with their paper bodies
or gulped it quick with cans of beer or cast fishlines
through it or by it made cuisines or marshmallows and hot dogs
or made love away from it as though the sea could judge.

And in our wooden house, not far from two graveyards
flanking the short road in, my aging aunt and uncle
blessed the table meal and passed around the plates
of hot corned beef and cabbage, sweetened with potatoes,
carrots and onions and we peeled from our plates every
eatable ounce, which meant the corned beef and cabbage,
and abandoned the whole vegetable meal for someone else
to cry over. But my aunt was special: *eat everything*
or no dessert! And with disappointment raging through
our seasoned bellies like snipped snails, we finished the meal
with the whole hope of puddings puffed within our reach.

Then afterwards we, drowsy and excited around the table
while my aunt and uncle told stories of the Island as they
knew it twenty years before: of the off-Islanders who could
never qualify as natives, though they had lived there forever,
because they were not *born* Islanders; of the only murder the land
had ever known; of the trembling rooster-faced man who visited
too often in his alcoholic grief and who was once a famous
baseball star; of the sea, and fishermen spawning into the
Atlantic mornings at sunrise; of the dead who lived not far
away; of the corruption of the Island by tourists:
(Was I one?)

And once a hurricane boomed into the bowels of the Island
and exploded it to shrouds and shreds and my uncle,
old and once a carpenter, harboring deep hostilities against
the Portuguese princes, craftsmen hardier than he, and one
his neighbor, sat jubilantly while the sacrilegious wind
scorched the tin top of the garage next door from its
roots and swung it to shelter his shaggy truck helpless
under a tree: *God is good! God is good!* he shouted, his hands like
buoys crusted with sea-salt, a forefinger long since sacrificed
for some winged chair soothing a summer estate, his hands
swivelling in the hysterical air, his feet clapping the rotted
wood of the porch so it shook, causing my mother to say an extra
prayer because in the deepest part of the house, where silence
was sane, she thought the frenzy was the hurricane.

Look how he protects my property with my enemy's!
And the storm razed and heckled and quieted and ran away.
In the morning a terrible wash of blue flushed into
the Island by the storm's torment and grace; the busy sun
anxious to repair the rain's ruin, bits and pieces
of drowned land split under its energy; skiffs
and trawlers, dingies and yachts and schooners bitten into
by the hurricane's hunger and left floating or run aground
like last week's leftovers; and yet the brilliance
of the afterday, crackling like fresh fire, gentle.

So, the end of summer; the flour fights, where one
hits his opponent over the head with the whitest
of flours and before his wits return, pastes him in
water; my mother's telling of turkeys that die in rain;
swans creaming the pond in swan-straight lines,
the boy who raised the bridge for sailboats or anything
high, late on a foggy evening, the harbor deserted, hollow
in his open hands; three gulls motionless a few feet apart,
watching derelict winds; the evening meal and laughter
at my uncle's heavy stories of purity and courage;
the strong listening of my aunt, whose arms had once
held deer she had hunted to keep her family from
starvation during the depression and whose smile now
seemed to remember wrens and lilacs; and all the goodnights,
the anointment of stars, the sudden smell of beaches
in soft black air.

Now, they are gone.
They died in their shrunken and tired visions
and their absolving joy. Their swift deaths
came dumb like afternoons when little things
of season slipped unnoticed; and there is no
geography now to bear the hermit's laughter
or kill the hurricane or silence the tongue-scalding
hot tea and lemon syrup after a chill or an
occasional cough of cloud or sneeze of rain or
footnote the complaint of fog-horns and the grip
of gulls groaning in wind; or reach the stoney pain
of their singular and sacramental endurance
upon that holy fragment of New England sea.

Uncle Gus

Gus would sit at his piano:
Oh, how he played his Ghost Rags!
(which were written by somebody else).

The piano jumped and swooned,
shimmied around the middle,
made fun of his fingers

that were too fat to hit all
the right notes at the right time.
Two keys together: one wrong,

one right, what did it matter?
Gus had his long, lonely singing
song, drifting through his rich

black body like his mother's
homemade molasses. He sat
proudly playing in his little

parlor for his family: his nieces,
nephews, mothers and sister
(his pa long gone, dead of alcohol

and debt), Gus, himself, a borrower
of sorts, now and then a little
borrowing from all those devoted

women, his good lean body,
his high-stepping legs, all in
greystriped pants, his strong chest

breathing through the white, crisp
shirt and black tie, the gold tie-pin
with a dust of diamond glimmering

in the afternoon light, as he took
his best step toward the piano again.
Sitting more upright than the music,

Uncle Gus ragged the piano to tin-cup
begging, reached for the cool glass
of his mother's wine on the edge

of the piano, sipped, danced in his seat,
laughed at the goodness of his rhythms,
and dared the ghosts to come.

Note to the Ophthalmologist

The apparatus is right:
It gleams properly flushing
Now into the night
Room that shines through seams

Of my eyeballs; screams
Of darkness don't matter:
Remember that. Whatever leans
Out of this eye is refuse

And prayer, the juice
Of retina poured from images
Only. The steely obtuse
Conversation between

Doesn't help at all. I mean
You Ophthalmologists are so helpless
After all. The best you glean
From my unclothed eye

Is sight; vision is high,
Too strong and deep for the big machine:
But instruments and scientists don't lie
And my hyperopia is a gift.

What is distance now is sift
From light, draining my gut (and backward).
Distance is liquid myopia, a lift
Into metals, forms, images, cold.

The eye of the storm
Is the window of my soul.

Bones Without Pockets

Never mind that last
touch of quail that
scampered down the
mountain as she heard
your footsteps;

or the chipmunk
that ran under the
wooden bridge when
your wavering shadow
reached its ears;

or the woodlilies
that died after
you picked them;
or the cook who
plunged from the castle

when the landslide
hit the mountain
and washed
the kitchen
into the sea;

or the man who jumped
in your dreams until
you were abandoned,
unidentified;

or the beggar who
spilled coffee
on your dress
when asking for
money for another cup;

or the swollen black-white
man who didn't know
his blood and picked
a revolution for you
instead of an afternoon
in his mother's house;

or the endangered species
of friends and family
who embrace one another
while words sour
on the table;

or the little lies
that mark the end
of a good book
or a straight poem;

or the hollows
in the ground
as you walk in
your thirty-dollar
shoes that are
already losing
their soles;

or the song that
never sings in the
night;

or the appetite
that is made from
too much disappointment.

Never mind all that.

The ghost is leaning
on the fence, her hands
dressed in pockets
of sweet night.

And your bones
are her deliverance.
Your matters
her celebration.

Pietà Negra*

Her face is like a hair of noon which glistens black
back into limbs of dreams and bones of her dry smile

which asks no questions, which is no lie
to eye the cold and stingy manger where swaddled

lies her shivering child in stiff and steely jaws,
claws of his jail cell hovering, which shut like headaches

streets and cities into the body of her brow;
for now the comely kings will walk, bearing hungry gifts

of death and life and absolution one of a time;
the crime of her sweet son: the will to be.

What she looks upon she anoints, and yet
to let the mother of her gaze, die too, is much a murder

as her deepened dead will, more precise than laws,
because she dies alone as he sinks in her lover's lap.

* *After the sculpture by Richmond Barthé: a Black woman holding her lynched son in her lap.*

The Devil Doesn't Always Come with Cloven Feet

He sat in my stomach.
And without moving from his
Chair, put tidily in the corner
Of my belly, he offerd me a martini.
I refused. *I don't like martinis,*
I said. *I don't drink.* With this
Wild courage drawn from me, he sat
Upright and began to walk the
Floor of my throat with soft and
Silent ease and I began to admire
The fact that my throat could
Hold him. But then he found me out.

My throat grew chilly as he held
A wind whose slander broke my brain
Like a house in the eye of a hurricane.
There were noises of swift decisions,
Too swift to live in light, and I knew
He was crawling in the blood of my fear
At this passionless cocktail party (that
Was innocent) and before him my flesh
Peeled in fire. *Well then have a cup*
Of tea . . . .

I felt his watch in me as I took and
Sipped and I knew I drank his hatred.
But he moved me to act, as I sent his
Hatred to the pit of my stomach for
A courier. I wanted to be kind,
Yet my blood would not yield. *Coward,*
Take courage! he said. *Hate! And in*
The sweet softness of your body, which
I have seen, hate beautifully! Find a
Perfect hate to marry mine!

Something beside me was pressing close
For an answer, a nemesis. From the tongue
Of my tightened eyes, my hope leapt
To the heart of God. I felt the Being
Beside me move slightly forth and leave
A voiceless vacuum, dying fully like
The whisper of a meteor. Into this I
called: *I cannot hate the house because*
It surrenders to the hurricane.
That was all.

Opening my eyes I saw the pale, well-dressed
Woman with the cocktailed hand and frightened
Eyes, watching me. She could never be my
Friend, nor I hers. But I thought as
I handed her my empty cup, past the murmurs
Of the zombied crowd into which she willed
me: *I think I can catch you now.*

Eating in Nevada

In the morning
I come to the patio
a bowl of strawberries
in my hand,
some thought
of reading poems.

The liquid sun sugars
the grass like honey,
bees make love
to hollyhocks that bend
to the black butterfly
chasing summer ghosts.

Quail come to visit,
scatter their arias
among the olive trees,
and the fleshy mouth
of sky waking the day
with soft blue kisses.

I am at the foot of raw mountains,
I am within the bloom of mountains.

I eat a sweet warm
strawberry and with it
swallow a barrel
of marigolds. Pouring
the noon into my brain
like warm juices, I shed

another appetite until
the young smell of red
berries startles my vagueness,
gives hungers peace.
Losing the skin of metaphors,
I forget to read the poems.

In the Garden of Abednego

(for James Baldwin)

Nebuchadnezzar spake: At that time ye hear the sackbut, the harp, psaltery and symphony and all kinds of music, you shall fall down and worship the image I have made. . . .

He will deliver us out of thine hand, O king.
We will not serve thy gods nor worship the golden image
which thou hast set up . . . . . .

Nebuchadnezzar commanded that the furnace be heated seven times more than necessary . . . . . The fire had no power nor was a hair of their heads singed nor the smell of fire had passed on them . . . .

Daniel 3:4-7, 18, 46-50

The falling mortal is our brother!

Baldwin

No! I will not worship your gods!
(They are cold and passing,
formless and shrivelled,
no dust to speak of
no reflection in the sun.)

No! I will not give the sheep
to the fox or the crow
while he gouges out the eyes
of the lamb!

My garden is wise
(not little).

It sounds like
pharoahs in the night;

there are cypress here
and large rich lemons

and oranges that are bitter
and roses, dates, honeysuckle,
white grapes and sweet apricots,

the palms are higher
than the truth you cling to.
At night they sigh and linger
in my heart.

About me eat the stars
hungry at my footsteps
stumbling to God.

And the wind is soft
(and silly);
it dazzles the moon
high, high upon
the laughing hill.

And the moon makes
noises that you will
pray to hear one day
while I am in the furnace.

While my brothers
take themselves to my side
fixing their eyes upon
the sea that watered

their bones
while something
sang of their deaths.

Oh! but don't worry!
You will have your death!

(See the butterfly
drop by the grass?

See the sun
swallow the quivering
sky?)

And that must be,
will be, enough
for you, sad torturers!

For only the earth
will give back,
only God can
take life out of
the belly of a bone.

No! I will not bow
before the golden image!
I will not pass me
into a hereafter of flies
and worms, like the rotted figs
on the hillside.

Not me! Nor my brothers
whose mystery is your pardon,
whose beauty your disguise.

Give me the fire,
if that is all you have.
It's cheap, reliable,
it burns of itself
and casts no reflections.

It is modest, indiscriminate,
it laughs while it moves
into itself, there are no
moans in its consummation.

It is truth.

You do me well,
friends, masters,
you bless me as
I have never been
blessed:

in the mouth of God,

from the backs of my eyes
where vision is absurd
words deceive,
thoughts unmotion,
and all that is left
is grace.

That will do.
That will do well enough.

Taste the rain
for me, lonely ones.
It is for the grass,
it is for the mountain
and the lion, and all of us.
It is coming now.

Then afterwards,
kill it as you will.

The hope of God
can stand such murders.

Gethsemane A. D.

The Garden did not bloom
that year. It tossed its roots
into the open moon
emptied like shoots

of sunflowers drained from
a man's blood, sticking his eyes
until the rose that did not come
ached upon his mouth. The lies

were not his. (How could they be?)
They moved into the earth
like worms feeding tree to tree
changing death to birth.

The Man is gone, the Garden wide
awake with soothsayers' stones,
and if here a young man slightly died,
wept blood, offered bones

of his imagination to a kiss,
then blooms are out of place;
tomorrow he will ripe and rise,
release the terrible energy of his grace.

Hypertension

Being in love
may do it
or anger

craving the stars
may bring it
or waiting

listening to pain
may buy it
or looking at nothing

or arrogantly eating
junk memories
too fat and full

of calories
or the habit
of putting salt

on simple food.
When it comes
it is the blood

not the numbers
that counts
and seduces

If you're
a woman
it leaks.

Inuendoes: Six O'Clock News

Old Christopher placed his boy upon his lips.

He was strange, that boy,
I knew he'd come to no good,
Everything told me;
The house, the car he stole,
The streets.

Always, the streets.
Can't do anything about it now.
He's dead
In the street
In the morgue
In the undertaker's
In the church
In the ground
In me.

Twenty-five years of death
In him is dead.
He fought us all: me,
The House, the man with the
Badge, the streets,
His women. All.
Then he robbed that bank.
Saw it on T.V.
What good's a bank to me?
Did he die for that?

I wonder what white folks think
When their sons die nicely
In clean beds? I wonder if
Their guns and sons ever run
Together in their heads?
Well, I'm not crying because
I'm Black. No advantage in that.
But he's dead and Black and
Sprouting wings. That was his talent:

Stepping over the world like he was
Walking on air, arms spread apart,
Outward, chest swollen, visions
Slipping from his brain
Like tender meat.

Talent. Too much for him,
Too much for the regular world.
He simply lived beyond wings,
On promises, pain and suggestions.
Never said anything outright;
He only fussed and now and then
Was peaceful, perplexed, silent.

Sometimes I wake up early, about two or three,
And hear him crying in his crib.

Old Christopher thought suddenly of his angry wife
and said to all the watching, ailing strangers
squeezed into the bloodlight of Channel Three:
And that's right. That's right.

Cardinal in Summer

(for Regina)

The wise bird flies to the top of the wind
and wraps the steel cold morning to his breast;
but you bird I have seen
barred before my window, languishing

in the limp waxen sun
summer caught, fastened between the
steps of the venetian shade
(that cannot climb your heights

or break your flight and harbors
the white, stilled light at the blind
man's touch). What if some prowler
were to come, some eagle great

and treacherous, seeing life as death
and death as life, and unfree to choose?
Warm in the womb of the wind-tree,
red-warm yet quivering in shadow,

throat-warm, soft and cloud-warm
feather-branched in the small-boned world,
you rest,
and rocks below you crumble

into nests of scattered nothings
and the great wind-tree cries in dust
moves in heat, threads your song through
deathgreen fingers and sifts it to the

sound of silence
gripping little living things
stuffed away in watery cocoons:
What enemy is victor here?

Your will fizzes the universe.
What victory can there be
over you
in the nucleartime?

The fear is mine, bird,
the blind hold me.

Yet, I watch the blood on your
wing burn like fire and spring you
to the lap of God.

I Need These Tears

(Violetta in *La Traviata*)

go by
go by
the road
is not
travelled
yet;
the room
too narrow

go by.

take misery
with you;
(a true
companion)
and doubt
leave me

go by.

put a note
in the hall:
tack it
to the wall;
I will
read it
presently

go by.

I am
abandoned
and that
is good,
that is
honest:
the healing
is near,

the Love

the burn
in the eye

go by.

Against the Grain

(for Frank and Georgie Joest)

The wood was maple,
a small log
which he chain-sawed
to the figure
of an ancient African
man.

Nothing was lost,

not even the holes
made by worms
whose sound he heard
in the hollows of
his heart, through
the juices of the wood.

Then, he took the chisel,
struck and etched,
carved and discovered
rich veins of color:
designs, lines, balances,
the perfect harmonies
and baptisms.

Suddenly, the wood chipped,
distorted, asked a better
stroke, a different direction,
a finer matter. He responded,
turned the chisel in the
opposite direction, made
a new incision.

Such was his life,
his continuity. He could
not be against himself
when the merchants came to
call, or the fine Eastern
galleries danced around
his ring. So there
he was,

woodcarving his past into the future,
celebrating himself.

Now the wood was cauterized
and needed a healing, so he
brought the wood to light, to
soft exposures.

"I went against the grain,"
he said. "The wood will
not allow it: it will not
tolerate that kind of violence.
So, you see, I must turn
the other way, hit the piece
in the direction of the grain,
give it peace, possibilities
of its natural directions.
The wood will tell you what
to do. Follow its whisperings."

When the grain emerged,
strong and sure, unviolated,
in harmony with itself,
he smiled, and knew the
conclusions, the counting
of the new man, his origin,
his birth, his ordinary
pulse, throbbing in
the wood, in his small
deliverance.

Young Elias

Only the matters
of tears

the great smile
in the smooth cheek

the little tyrannies
that resemble
obediences

the games of the sea
the fretting of stars

the joy of the sound
of a father's
footsteps

a mother's mysterious
goings, comings
and embraces,
daylight for a mirror:

songs in sighs;

only these journeys
make him a child.

For My Father: on the gift of another eye

Now you have
another eye.
The one you had

wore out after
seventy-six years,
lost its strength,

its focus, its
sense of humor.
It could no longer

find its way
in the light.
It forgot how

to gasp. But
the operation
was a success:

(you took the rosary
though you and God
didn't play the same

horse and His tennis
was never as good
as yours) and you're

home again, alive,
with two fairly good
eyes, ready to resume

a fairly good business
with another fairly good
life in your pocket.

Your sight over the years
has really teased you,
led you to corners

when you needed
stairwells, wasn't
always to be trusted.

Even your visions
deserted you for awhile,
and you forgot how to weep.

And you were brave, honest:
you didn't complain. (I
admire you for that, that

was beautiful.) But this
eye given in the dark
by some secret person

may lead you into a blindness
that might be a gift beyond
a 20/20 dream: for suppose

the donor were a billiard
player, a fireman, a young
mother, or better still,

a magician? The possibilities
are stunning! though now
for a while you will be

in emptiness (no news is good);
angels will dance about
the rising retina, illusions

will enter your body
like water, colors will come
in prayers, peaceably enforced,

sound will slip into your brain
with slippers on. Gloucester will
weep in your closet. (You will give

him a silver dollar for ice-cream.)
Yet nothing will be disturbed.
Not really. The matters of men

under calm recovery from
sleepwalking will all converge
on a single movement of the cornea,

a quiver in the clock,
and you, grand and unfinished,
the half-moon blooming

in your jaw, will in the night
whisper your tired and galloping
visions to a second sight.

Yielding

(for Parrish and Peyton Houston)

We talked of graves and music and sad men sleeping on
water and the night spawning of stars in sudden sky We
talked of light and the fire that grew in the cave of
the house as ice grew in the cave of the river of flowers
as geraniums bloomed in the cave of windows Our voices
were fires larging in the easing dusk and the yellow cold
sky that dared to heat the horizon The ice on the river
stiffened as we lit poems like dry wood on our tongues
and the geraniums slipped brighter poems into the air
we later warmed with our last listening to the dark But
dark was yet to come the strain of metaphors was yet to
lift into the last light Something was dying out there
across the river Something alive was in death and singing
The sunset had a coffin of grey within it and the clouds
wore mute satins of slender reflections We silenced
ourselves in respect out of stunned words unable to
rise to the occasion We smiled at our absurdity in such
an evening We let the fire burn forgot the geraniums
as they closed their open red mouths over their dim
room and watched a flock of ducks move down the river
on a thin boat of ice (Our windows were our persons)
Suddenly they flew

Next morning the white dark came and slumbered in the
wind It left grains of snow on doorsills ballustrades
glass and rock It smoothed the pines to bone and made
everything identical and hard I watched the black ducks
talking from the ice to one another as whiteness lifted
from dark like tiny voices broken between cold shafts of
air I heard the ducks grieve saw them puff their bodies
into lumps of shadow as if to sustain their line felt
their strange grief-song move into the water that carried
it under ice to towns along the Sound Then without warning
the sun cut through their antiphons and cleaned the sky
of everything but ghost stars and yellow light And me
in my room without apologies opened doors wiped the
fragile windows of the cold made a liar of grief Too
quickly the ducks were gone to gulls that rose into the
throat of the last echo of light Yielding in the late
winter air a little softness melted on a bowl of oranges

An Opening of the Veins

(for Betty Uston)

note: from the uncommon unconscious to the 10:20 am class

You want me to be your friend, your limb of light, your skeleton
of grace, your loose and unstilled honored melancholy thumping
from the heart; you want my bone in roses, the flow of heat
in loosened skin, the thrift of grief in fingers gripping books
and dumb pulses of killed afternoons murdered by chalkdust.
You want an opening of the veins, holy blood; but your needs
come close to what holiness used to be because you want me to see
you as sacred, faulty without fault. That is my Job, my Profession,
my Calling, my Vocation, my Pedagogy.

And you? Where is your rough blood? Has the world so taken,
so stolen, so ravished you that your life is sprung from
mine alone? Are we the new society? The new cannibals? We handle
words, tease and talk, disguise our only selves in sounds that we
create to smother thoughts, and in all this we violate life. You
do not wish to suffer, so you exact it before it is due by manipulating
the fall guys. You curse the system, but how we both know that even
as you drop your paradigms of pain, you feed your veins into the Big
Machine that calls you closer, closer, ever closer! Your inheritance
is inevitable.

Your thin power struts in wind; your eyes and dreams are put
safe-by, in storage, monthly rental, cold and dark, boxed
in moth-balls, no interest, no account. I wish I could blame
your helplessness on The Establishment, Education or Me.
But that's been done before. Don't you see? Whoever are the meek
will inherit the earth. And. The earth is round, bulging in space
between stars, apogee and perigee, crossing after clouds and clops
of rain, flowers and your feet in mud or dust. Walk it ever.
Your hands hold it, your fists clench it, your fingers grip it.
(You walk what you behold.)

Yet, one day, it will explode and only the meek
who warm an asteroid of honor in their jaws will smell
the noise before the fire, put the sign of the ram,
our last language, upon the door,

and know.

There Is No First Time

(for Angél Vilalta)

There is no first time:
only the image
only the place
and the pause.

No windows that see,
no iron bars that rust,
no rain that softens,
no sun that leaks.

Always the memory
and the forgetfulness,
the horror and the crime,
the last lover leaving

as the sour breaking
disappears into your sleep,
bearing his skin on your voice,
watching his obediences;

or the large dream walking
through the cupboard, that
is now peeling and cracked
and dry and needs cleaning.

There is no first time:
only what is newly given,
what is true, only
the stranger's borrowing.

Scaling the World Trade Building

It is
high
and he
can
make it
in an
era.
The windows
mount
nothing
but
his dream
climbs
deep
into the
universe
touches
its
belly
with a
steel star.
Grab it
he can.
Watch
the windows
now!
They break
too
(under
specified
pressure).
Up
past
the
second
floor;
then the
fourth
fifth
eighth
eleventh.
Disregard
the
unnumbered
one.
Thirteen
doesn't
exist
in
megaphones
of power.
Touch
the twelfth
gently
deeply
as lungs
of air
come
cleaner
purer.
Push
in blue
lumps of
height
stiffening
eyes
to outerworlds
of power
where trade
is meridian
to merchants
hooting
like owls
dumb of
sight
(because
as he
goes
all fall
down).
Up! Push!
To the top!
the mountain
isn't enough!

The ache
of ascent
won't peaceably
rise upon
rocks
and valleys
crevices
of storms
high winds
and rhythms
of the mind;
conscience
traded
for concrete
plastics
comfortable
lighting
(of course
indirect)
the world.
See! Humans
work in
cubicles
of solar
storms
and think
that it's
a nine
to five
job!
The building
now is
resilient
moves
sways
climbs
with him
takes him
to its
chest
scratches
his hunger
with fingers
that feel
like bread
to calm
his willing
appetite.
The building
is like
a mountain.
It stands
high
everything
becomes
its shadow
even its
fabric
that is
rough and
without static.
How tame
his winds
are!
How much
sky
there is
to be killed!
How surly
his winds
are!
How brazen!
Dare *they*
whip him
from his
first
lovemaking
to a power
living
within
their own?
Are they
jealous?
No.
The mountain
is. Beyond
his grip,
beyond the
trade of
sun kicking
through clouds
for a world
flashing
loneliness
in sprawls

atop
Manhattan,
touching
concrete
instead
of granite
glass
instead
of snow
mortar
instead
of water,
he quivers,
hesitates;
the burn
of solar
winds
turns
his scaling
insideout
masterminds
his stretching
neck and arms;
thin strategems
of crumbling
curls of air
embrace him.
breath
that is
short
now is
divided
rationed.
A God
out there
somewhere
waiting
for the
water
in his eyes
to fix
streams
and lakes
in high
sierras.

Suddenly
he is
a high
sierra
coloring
daylight
in his
image.
Shutting
his sight
to the
climax
his hands
are granite
his legs
rocks
his feet
roots
of all
that is
tall
and vulnerable
his toes
trees
coming
of age.
The ascent
is only
as high
as he
stretches.
Now!
Fixing
himself
like a
monument
upon
the top
he watches
grids
of people
pushing
ceremonies
up into
a permanence

of stars
and what
is natural
what is
sweet.
He lingers
in the
universal
moment
for one
terrible
devouring
exhaustion
looks about
wonders
believes
unbelieves
knows
the climb
is his own
casualty
of hope
knows
that climbing
creates
climbing
not
immortality
knows
his own
communion
with
the way up
has only
given
him
the way
down
knows
the silence
of tricks
the gentleness
of giants
the trade
of sudden self
for small
asteroids
of honor
and the longing
of little men.

We Are the Writing on the Wall

We are the writing on the wall
our Black dynasties of blood
running into stone

the young alphabet of our grief
stronger than the whines of citizenry
stalking us alone

with nostrils wide like pumas
pacing their impatient properties.
We are the bone

of that daylight squatting in the dark
sealed in the absolution of tombs;
the hieroglyphic home.

And Olaf, Too

(for Martin)

Christ (in His mercy infinite)
i pray to see; and Olaf, too

preponderatingly because
unless statistics lie he was
more brave than me: more blond than you.

"i sing of Olaf" by e. e. cummings

I.

Christ: expedient

It is expedient that one man should die for the people.

struggles the whip moves in seasons reasons

to give a little relax just a little

remember *it* profits a man nothing to gain urbane

logic through bones of brittle grief

sweat it out whatever *is expedient* will expedite fight

its way beyond *that one* cause that last

and final *man*; *should* causes growl and cease increase

the appetites of laws and terrible men

die under out around beyond because laws

for the people usually cancel themselves out among

the rags of worn tradition clothing beggars and lovers others

merely make love And you you You.

II.

Conscientous: ProtestOr

Nukes

If we care about humankind, he said, we will not live
beside this newest dragon, this fertile beast that
calls the nuclear rape into his appetite

with words of quick and cheap survival. Coughing up our holy
blood through loosened teeth of money, we will take this
monster wearing like vests his casual tongues of smooth

synthetic fibers absorbing sweat from sour drastic skin, unclothe
him, move him out into the naked universe, show him
energies as yet unconsulted, drop the awful

plainness of his metaphor that drowns in his own fire sprouting
worms into one square mile of God and satisfy his lust for
little powers by making pure his breath.

Thus saying past his own uncluttered breathing, he faced
the crumpled court, the crimson judge his parent and
his child, and for all his kin (his enemies included)

took ritual of whatever prisons warmed in wait.

The Painter in Seasons

(for Bud)

Summer

He is sweet
in the warm flesh
of bright rooms
that cover his eyes
with murmuring brushes
and answering lilacs.

Autumn

The wizards come
in soft winds,
rains that melt
his fingers into oxides
cleaning color from air,
strangely felt.

Winter

I don't like cold,
he thinks, and pushes
aside the lemon star
squeezed in the corner
of his canvas, inside
his shivering sky.

Spring

What blooms
is his thin soul
formed from nothing,
shattering light,
protecting the seasons
of his hands, waiting.

Ge

I think when you
took me to Mass

that fine day
and we did not know

each other's language
and your shy French

was as casual
as my English

we became friends
leaning through the ribs

of our common
heritage, and Paris

had little to say
to us, had nothing

to say or whisper
or breathe, except

your youngness, growing
in your small and angular

body, twelve years
out of an African covenant.

As we moved together
into the narrow streets

where Africans in Paris
slip into their homelands

in the robe of a noun,
you moved ahead, leading,

sure of your way,
man of your house,

boy of your sweet
and busy heart.

The Mass was familiar,
and we heard it well;

then we went
to a patisserie

for croissants
and the lemon tart

you most enjoyed
when sharing was not

part of the eating.
Later we gave our silence

to one another because
our tongues were intruders,

that morning
we dared to make holy.

Night Fragments

Creases of memory made by the dark,
actors diminished
day light assembled
dog in the howl of the street's last sun
dreams awakened one by one
as accidents might.

You.
And yet, the roof of your arms
wrung 'round me like sleep
soft in the bloom of another's sake
keeping the clocks from running awake
held to a last new light.

Resurrection Bum

(for Mary DeVault)

phrasing

This morning
I got up
in the dark,
dressed, heard
my stomach rattle,
while dead leaves
sank in the river.

rising

I want a handout,
alms (no cost);
my belly is swollen,
my mouth calloused,
my bones too heavy
for my skin. There's
a letter in my room
somewhere: it speaks
of good wishes
and a legacy I'd
forgotten. I read it
again. For enough
of a moment, my belly
flattens, my mouth cools,
and my skin puts wings
to my bones.

Dead Asters

(for Cabot Lyford)

Crumbling. Dry before water.
Make my bed. Cream my cup.
Sweet. Into the final lip.
A fresh pail of afternoon.

Crumbling. A favorite stem.
All crust upon water.
Dust my table. Stand in state.
(And who will mourn for you?)

Crumbled. The last day.
Metamorphosis like final rites:
Red to rose, purple to mauve.
Green to stiff prayers of leaves.

A gasp of color.
Outside, it rains.

Blue Dan

our havings are our cleansing

I.

And when the day is your enemy,
and you are swollen with hatred
from an invisible cause
and your dangling body swells,
no hoisting to its favor
no energy to its weight:

II.

Blue Dan stands behind the post-clerk's counter,
his music issuing rhythms as colorful
and finely-crafted as the stamps he sells.
Blue Dan's music is his companion,
the Bach of mid-day balancing on Virgil's
organ like a high-wire act, saturates
the stale and ugly room.

III.

A fugue: flight: distances.

IV.

I'd like ten stamps, I say.
I am not intelligent on a day like this.
I am untendered to hope,
the paucity of havings.
I'd like ten twenty-cent stamps, I say.

V.

Blue Dan plays Bach: the portable stereo
is lovelier than I. He gives me the stamps
and talks to me about Fox and Bach. There are
30,067 pipes on the organ and 451 stops.
Bach leaps through each one like a tiger,
but he's really just having a good time;
he's found an ecstasy and he's somewhat ravenous,
what a wonder! He's on both sides of joy at the same
time, and for him the way is smooth. Oh, each
one of these pipes is dangerous on a bad day!

VI.

Blue Dan remembers:

My days are numbered.

I am mellow.

I am royal.

I am without death.

Sometimes Bach enters

my skin like a thief.

He never knocks.

VII.

And when the day is your enemy,
you search for weapons and find
instead grace rising in brief rooms
like a lost sorcerer.

Something in Passing

We walked the back route
into the town; you didn't
notice my awkwardness
under a well-trained
confidence, my little
noisy conversation
designed to protect me
from a fragility I thought
had left me years ago.

You, too, needed to feel
the solid concrete under
your feet, the distance
of where the walk would
lead, and gave such distance
only careful words, little
homages that would melt
in the evening air, like
the wings of fireflies.

We passed the town graveyard
where two young men stopped us
and urged that we watch the
cemetery sparkle as the winged
creatures carried their fire
ritually around mounds
of tombstones hanging loosely
in the rich and cauterized night.

I thought we needed to touch,
to know ourselves more honestly,
to praise ourselves with fire
that came out of the dark and danced.
"That's never happened around here
before," one of the two young men
said. "Never?" we asked. "No."

You watched the dance
with a special power, now.
It was yours and mine
and his and hers
and light and dark
and earth and air
and bothersome questions
flying about in insects.

We moved down the grassy path
slowly, looked back to give
the young men a thanks
as they sat silently beside
the gate bearing the Word,
all those who enter here
must smile and rest and come
in peace.

And we knew our destination;
we were separating, moving
into magic distances where
plurals could not exist.
Something had happened:
we had glimpsed a secret
of the immortal Now,
and as strongly as it had
come it gave us choices
which we accepted by walking
uneasily away.

There was Venus with
a companion star, seen only
once in every twenty-five
years. You talked of
science-fiction: I talked
of independent women.
Behind us the burning
profiles of the young men
glowed, their heads wrapped
in loose bandannas, blue jeans
on their bodies, and wings.

ABOUT THE AUTHOR

Dolores Kendrick was born in Washington, D.C., and taught in the public schools there before accepting her present appointment as instructor in English at The Phillips Exeter Academy. As a 1963 Fullbright Fellow in Belfast, Northern Ireland, she adapted Dickens' *A Christmas Carol* to the talents of her students, all of whom were girls. She also adapted this novel into a musical play which the *Belfast Telegraph* described as having "a distinct Irish flavor." Upon her return to this country, Ms. Kendrick won an experienced teacher fellowship to Georgetown University where she received her MAT degree. She has also taught at Iolani School in Honolulu, Hawaii, and recently in Barcelona, Spain.

In 1965, Ms. Kendrick's narrative poem, "Freddie," won the Deep South Writers' Award and has since been performed at the Folger Shakespeare Library. During the Fifties, she was editor and frequent contributor to *Dasein.* Her work has appeared in many literary quarterlies, anthologies, and poetry magazines, including *Freeing the Spirit, Nethula Journal, The Washington Review, Washington Dossier, four quarters, To Gwen with Love,* and *The Beloit Poetry Journal,* among others. While she was in Ireland, her work was published in the popular Belfast quarterly, *The New Republic.*

Through the Ceiling, Ms. Kendrick's first collection of poetry, was published in 1975 in London by Paul Breman. In 1981, she was poet-in-residence at Holy Cross College, Worcester, Massachusetts, and guest lecturer that summer at the annual writers' conference at the University of Rochester. During the same year, she read at The Library of Congress, where her work has also been recorded in its Contemporary Poets Series.

The author presently divides her time between Exeter, New Hampshire, and Washington, D.C.